Fun in the Sun

Addition

Lisa Greathouse

Consultants

Chandra C. Prough, M.S.Ed.
National Board Certified
Newport-Mesa
   Unified School District

Jodene Smith, M.A.
ABC Unified School District

Publishing Credits

Dona Herweck Rice, *Editor-in-Chief*
Lee Aucoin, *Creative Director*
Chris McIntyre, M.A.Ed., *Editorial Director*
James Anderson, M.S.Ed., *Editor*
Aubrie Nielsen, M.S.Ed., *Associate Education Editor*
Neri Garcia, *Senior Designer*
Stephanie Reid, *Photo Editor*
Rachelle Cracchiolo, M.S.Ed., *Publisher*

Image Credits

cover MaszaS/Shutterstock; p.3 Shutterstock; p.4 caracterdesign/iStockphoto; p.5 goldenKB/ iStockphoto; p.6 (top) Studio 1One/Shutterstock, (bottom) Arvind Balaraman/Shutterstock; p.7 Shutterstock; pp.8–9 (top) BigStockPhoto, (bottom) khz/Shutterstock; pp.10–11 (top) MaszaS/ Shutterstock, (bottom) Golden Pixels LLC/Shutterstock; p.12 (top) Beata Becla/Shutterstock, (bottom) fotohunter/Shutterstock; p.13 Shutterstock; p.14 (top) Elena Elisseeva/Shutterstock, (bottom) Alex Bramwell/iStockphoto; p.15 Shutterstock; p.16 (top) Carmen Martínez Banús/iStockphoto, (bottom) YinYang/iStockphoto; p.17 (left) Mircea BEZERGHEANU/ Shutterstock, (right) karen roach/Shutterstock; p.18 (top) Dmitry Naumov/Shutterstock, (bottom) BigStockPhoto; p.19 Stephanie Reid; p.20 (top) Steve Bower/Shutterstock, (bottom) BigStockPhoto; p.21 Shutterstock; p.22 (top) Peter Booth/iStockphoto, (bottom) P72/Shutterstock; p.23 JeniFoto/Shutterstock; p.24 Stacie Stauff Smith/Shutterstock; p.26 IKO/Shutterstock; p.28 Jani Bryson/iStockphoto

Teacher Created Materials

5301 Oceanus Drive
Huntington Beach, CA 92649-1030
http://www.tcmpub.com
ISBN 978-1-4333-3433-7
© 2012 Teacher Created Materials, Inc.
BP 5028

Table of Contents

The sun is out.

Time to cool off!

1 tube

1 tube

6

Add!

$$1 + 1 = 2$$

There are 2 tubes in **all**.

1 slide

2 slides

Add!

$$1 + 2 = 3$$

There are 3 slides in all.

3 kids

2 kids

Add!

$$3 + 2 = 5$$

There are 5 kids in all.

2 pinwheels

4 pinwheels

Add!

$$2 + 4 = 6$$

There are 6 pinwheels in all.

3 beach balls

5 beach balls

Add!

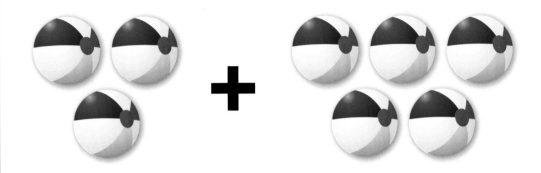

$$3 + 5 = 8$$

There are 8 beach balls in all.

1 sea star

6 sea stars

Add!

$$1 + 6 = 7$$

There are 7 sea stars in all.

1 water toy

7 water toys

Add!

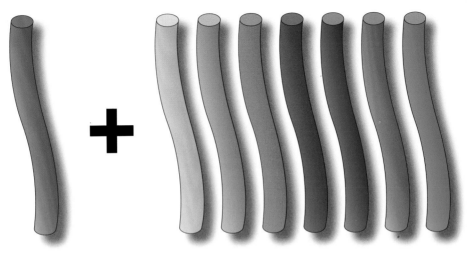

$$1 + 7 = 8$$

There are 8 water toys in all.

2 kites

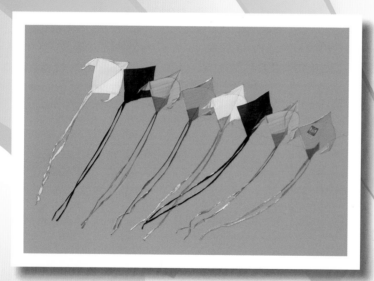

8 kites

Add!

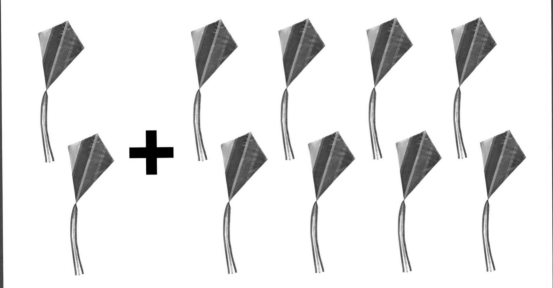

$$2 + 8 = 10$$

There are 10 kites in all.

1 shell

9 shells

Add!

$$1 + 9 = 10$$

There are 10 shells in all.

How many toys in all?

4 beach toys

6 beach toys

Add!

+

4	+	6	=	

0 — 1 — 2 — 3 — 4 — 5 — 6 — 7 — 8 — 9 — 10

How many surfboards in all?

3 surfboards

5 more surfboards

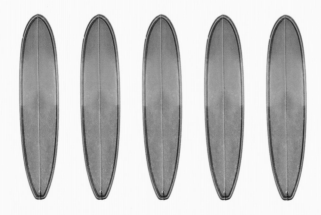

Add!

How many jumping jacks can you do?

Materials
✓ number cards 0–5
✓ pencil
✓ paper

1 Pick a number card. Do that many jumping jacks.

2 Pick another card. Do that many jumping jacks.

3 Add. Write a number sentence to show how many jumping jacks you did in all.

0 1 2 3 4 5 6 7 8 9 10

Glossary

add—to find how many things there are in all

all—the whole amount

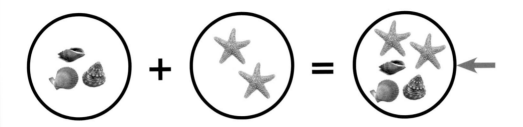

You Try It!

Pages 24–25:
4 + 6 = 10
There are 10 beach toys in all.

Pages 26–27:
3 + 5 = 8
There are 8 surfboards in all.

Solve the Problem

Answers will vary.